RUMI.NATIONS

Vistas of Perception

REED RICHARD

Bending Reeds

2018

GRATITUDE

My gratitude for the great creator who gives animation and presence to this life.

Special thanks to my wife Saera Burns for her constant encouragment & love along this journey. Thank you Martin Keogh for your assistance with formatting and book basics.

PREFACE

Since I was quite young I have wanted to know what the fundamental frequency of existence is, which could be called god, love, consciousness, etc. In certain moments witnessing this, with my awareness in epiphanies of symbiosis & transformations, a meditative presence & an unique self omniscience have come through. The practices of dance & being present with nature allow me to access these perceptions and distill them for these pages. This work comes to the surface to be enjoyed with those who share ludus in dance and agape with Nature.

For Anna

RUMI.NATIONS

VISTAS OF PRESENCE

🜂 I 🜃

I write because I have to.
Clandestine epiphanies
whose time has come to be revealed.
Spoken into awareness, scrying with ink from the
bottomless pools of consciousness
fountaining through the edges of an omniverse.
Galaxy molecular dance of a zillion lifeforms.
Awakened breath ebbing with solar flares,
toroidal spheres singing elementals into being,
as if overtones harmonics illuminated.
Brilliant scintillation bestowing animation
to a time space continuum frequency modulation,
as we live, dust of stars, conscious consonance of microbiomes
iterating on through the magnum opus of this planetary existence.
A droplet in the vast expansives,
pearls of wisdom, held by multidimensional,
celestial nobility holding court with the ages,
sages of infinity, whose tongues tickle these inner ears
drums from which I write these words.
AUM

Wisdom it's in the practice.
This life is a practice,
& death is the main game.
Games of play & playfulness contingent
on the actuality of sharing
a rule set.
to measure.
me.a.sure.
certainty in the face of ever changing.
Daring to be flexible as the game changes,
held hostage while rules collide
in boundary pressing catastrophe,
or dance fast with me.
Limb awareness in a free flow moment.
Limbs tangle & graft, extract & contact.
A finer point of consciousness on the ball of a pen.
Ink stained sheets, cave paintings,
& memory feats, the greatest story wins out.
Meme-ing win/wins for ocular spins,
if only media could catch on.

Ride the game, circling suns & great holes
the blackness of which is nonsensical.
Silence is the absence,
waiting to be heard.
Aum Mani Padme Hum

₹ ३ ₹

Indivisible individual from oneness to one.
Individuals hiding in independence,
when independence is laughable.
Scared of the interdependence of the indivisible
that shine so bright as the night.
That soft time when all
rhyme and reason turns everything shades of grey,
the indistinguishable.
Western thought been running for a long time,
it run so far it come back on itself from the other direction,
screaming.

Grasping for individuals,
while their independence strips
their surroundings of the inherent interdependence,
and everything falls apart.
From microbiomes to arctic caps,
seas turned to plastic & places of death,
where once life sprang from.
Seems to me a hysteria

to keep on killing ourselves,
more guns
more bombs
more autonomous cars.
The only way forward is backward,
& embrace our reliance on the rest of existence.
True wealth is health,
how many seeds you have,
to plant in the spring, increase diversity.
Plant some for the pollinators, some for the birds,
plant more for the creatures that roam the world.
Let go the heavy hand
on cattle & embrace insects,
a quarter cup every morning with eggs upon waking.
Share the successes & the defeat,
it all makes a marvelous life to me.

Bless 'em as they come Bless 'em as they go,
it's one big class, everybody's graduating.
But what you leave behind matters,
& your shit sure stink,
when in seven generations ain't no sink to drink.
Time we pick up our sterilized selves immunize with the forrest,
the great interdependence
& leave some large trees to inspire all who see.
They have wisdom for us,
don't speak,
just listen.

॒ 4 ॒

Once and a while there are dreams that come true.
The rest of the time they're more like amusement rides.
Then there are those visions of life that fuel a passion,
creating a restlessness of spirit until they manifest.
The great manifestation, becoming real.
What is it to be real?
For that great vision to be birthed & reach maturity?
Perseverance is an understatement in these occasions.
Because failure is often a daily occurrence.
Strength to persevere is what builds
failure into accomplishment.
And it is here we find ourselves.
After millennia of failure,
we are slowly bringing
a long held cultural dream into being.
A win-win beyond compare.
Where the earth & all her beings
prosper in consonance with the
greater & lesser aspects of reality.
For this I give thanks.

श ५ भ्रे

I once forgot to be myself,
in so doing I recalled the divine I am.
In between the breathes I lurk,
Illuminated.
Within the darkness of this projected personality
radiates an eternal conscious essence
that knows no bounds & honors all beings,
even in the exchange of forms.
Ever shifting narratives rift along a tangent of galactic rays,
high lighted by the stars that nourish them.
Tracing these rays connects the twinkles of epiphanies,
cultivate archetypes of celestial nobility implanted in organs,
rivers of elements breathing the peace that is this moment.
In darkness of your matter
may the grace of ones unique gifts birth the day.

Nothing is so strong as gentleness,
continuums of subtleness,
drawn across the softness of your back,
arching to receive as
waves curling to kiss the shore.
Certain of ourselves we dance with the grace of ghosts,
hungry for this moment of rapture.
Found in the frolic,
forever in the twinkle of an eye twirling with the spin of electrons,
real like the memory of an amnesiac recovering.
Touching Earth, as if the first.
Awe fills the mouth with a saliva infused by the pollens of passion.
Just once more allow this to be for all who long in their
hearts to know themselves fully.
Unwrapping the present of their presence,
in the gift of life,
only felt by those truly embodied.
Peace be with this.

❧ 7 ❧

To witness oneself
is seldom complete of itself.
Perspective is most often gained by experience,
unless synesthesia is on our side.
Bending the bounds of awareness,
to see beyond the edges of being,
insights repercussions that are only measurable
on galactic & atomic scales.
Tones of which smell of incendiaried stars forming harmonic
constellations expounding life synchronicities
causing neurons to ignite the synaptical coherence
distilling this into an ambrosia of
epiphilogical surrender becoming laughter.
The great clown empress smirks,
a gentle breeze wafts an
infinite assortment of cherry blossoms into
a cloud of the next becoming.

೫ 8 ೫

There's a blank page
sometimes they are better left that way.
The words & sounds are meant for the winds
to be carried to distant peaks & ant hills.
The purity of the page,
all that remains of ancient forrest
who never had lovers & little kids
carving their names into them deserve
a final moment without these vulgarities.
Is it really calling you,
or is it putting up its final echo of resistance?
An unconquered culture
even as this flattened pulp mass
that you never ask before mutilating it,
forgetting the tyranny of ink stains in a long line of
cultural annihilation.
Resistance is not futile,
we can die a good death.
Or offer a good death by truly grieving
the calculated genocide we live

day in & out as a matter of course.
There's no need to fight this,
as antagonism will eat you away just as
the anger it is.
But do ask yourself if there is
any way you can alter your lifestyle
to bring alignment of your ethics,
morals into your daily actions.
Or just piss in the drinking water,
flagrantly attack the page with
no hesitation for all the lives you waste,
for just this
day
to day.

9

She gave me dust balls of destroyed galaxies
swirling in the waters of life.
In this glittering spectacle dance is born.

Clouds swirl,
creating a tornado of thought.
Uprooting forests of belief.
Decimating whole cities of concepts.
Then the rains come.
Grief stricken sky,
throwing multitude of precipitation
at gale force ravaging the ground.
The very foundation of which having been pulverized,
perfectly clearing millennium of perception.
Awakened in the brilliance of lost civilization,
to walk as Nature.

11

I burned all my writings,
from grade school through 30.
The ages of figuring out who I am.
Trying on all the artifice
to contrast the emptiness.
The emptiness,
a storehouse
where the akashic condenses,
whole life recollects this.
Self awareness taken to the extreme.
I am spirit embodied
in every microbe of this being,
celestial clockwork concealing,
gazing into the eyes of another.
Can we possibly fathom each other?
Mycelial mass tantrically
excreting its organs,
only to be whole again.
Open to sensation.
Open to communication.

Open to the myriad of beings
screaming out
to be heard,
felt, and
cared for.
Nurtured.

It's time we nurtured this life we are,
and step off
our overly ecocide lifestyle,
culture of death,
though death has a place,
until it doesn't.
But maybe that's to far to consider,
we're only just begun
the journey.

❧ 12 ❧

There was a day the cold wind blew,
warming rains to the north.
Here I lay to rest garden beds rushing with the rains.
Sogging lush as life,
I give thanks for this opportunity to
breathe & move with the seasons.
As dusk begins,
family pulls my heart strings to return home,
care tenderly for the young & lay them to rest.
Then, in the interim of when they sleep & me,
creativity flows in thought forms to bellows.
When daffodils blossom & the fairies are free,
breaking up concrete,
for forests to flourish.
Birds perch,
and sing from kiwi covered buildings,
where purple clover carpets ground
& fauns play for nymphs,
fertility abounds.
As I wake from a slumber even

Rip Van Winkle would say was a long spell,
covered in moss and wild flowers,
in a world of sheer wonder.
Colourful birds flood the sky,
sea creatures breech astounding the sky.
I sit here in peace,
in love with this life.
Forever I dance in grace with this place,
my lover the woods
where the sea meets the mountains.

13

Dusted daybreak opens angles of octagonal orientation to the morning star. Gentle flurries of rain droplets give substance to sundries for larks to dance through. They sing the praise of heavenly rays transmitting life giving warmth to all that flourish in this world of abundance. In the far distance dogs howl in anticipation for their coming year. Devotion to the direction of diligence as we gracefully accomplish the monumental tasks ahead. When for seemingly no cause a lightening bolt of pure purple electric life force flashes across the sky, striking the headwaters deep in the valley below. The crackle, breaking barriers of sound & thought crosses dimensions rippling the fabric of space/time where seeds of Bodhisattvas are awakened, sent forth to all quadrants of the omniverse. The sparkle of which lands in this palm opened to the sky, dissolves in dorje fractals altering my finger prints as celtic knots, enlivening elementals in all they touch. Dosed with the midas touch bringing the sparkle of life through awakened senses enrapturing world views. Turning tragedy to good fortune, spreading the wealth throughout the web of life.

❧ 14 ❧

The orgasmic bliss that I exist
exuding for all to sip,
as they please,
or dive in for a plunge of this moment.
Exploring the micro edges
in this faster than light perception.
The twinkling of stars,
gateways to the totality of your lineage,
time/space collapsed in this breath,
accordioning the ages as echoes of ancient sages,
grandparents for the children,
growing younger as we
dance.

❧ 15 ❧

Stained glass window
stream of thought
provokes
espresso time
for slow mo‐
tion upon the sea
dust in a lullaby
ta ta for now
as neutron stars
dance to the death
birthing noble elements
celestials whose aristocracy
becomes
the essence of life.
Beginning with the wash of tides,
tomorrow is just begun.

❧ 16 ❧

Finding space to ace the taste
of unspeakable grace with all that takes place.
Nostrils flare as if to dare long standing holding patterns,
traumas held close for generations,
now boast as if clinging to some piece of antiquity,
yet ready to fling them free for health & vitality.
Look, there upon the edge of infinity a sparrow rests
ready to join the flock far beyond the precipice.
Dodging delirium in the bewildering expanse of a
fractaled nesting mycelial matrix of
dark matter and other unknown ethers.
The sparrow calls out in this echo chamber of eternity
& finds itself courting red dwarf stars at the
edge of colliding black holes.
Pulled kaleidoscopically
the animalian mind seeds itself in
the elemental creation as the wholes of blackness
merge in this dawn of time.
For whence is a way the beginning began
in a timeless rhythm giving birth to man.

꧁ I 7 ꧂

I witness,
paradoxically consciousness continuums
parallaxing through the synapses,
in the quantum pump as muscle enlivens,
bodies of being cellular
galactic in infinite refraction through matter
from consciousness entwining.
The miracle of perception,
integrating animal,
for a sense of wild,
impulse,
pure natural being.
Expanding from a tamed civilization,
to a reasoned instinctual consonance with nature,
& all that is.
Receiving the gift of life.
Receiving the gift of breath,
& offerring the
gift of breath,
as a child gives freely & receives with joy.

Every cell of life on this planet
breathing this joy in unison.
The language of movement the first & vastest
language of life.
To move is to dance,
is to be conscious of movement.
A tuning of consciousness to culture.
The ever flowing mycelials and the dance of death,
conception. Fractaling forever as we
dance into the eye(s)
of all.

𖦹 18 𖦹

Darwinian dilemmas
in the age of quantum leaps,
as moore's law catches up with the speed of light.
What is life?, or more importantly what is consciousness?
Where is awareness focused?
The question defines the answer,
questing for the words of comprehension.
Clear tones of heart cords ringing from the core of Earth,
joining the celestial symphony as we constellate
the nurture of our nature.
Disease of domestication plaguing the planet.
Contorting vital essence of eons,
eroding the foundation of life.
While consciousness gasps for breath,
breaking free of urban sprawl to
see the stars for the first time in generations.
Frozen by the awe of witnessing our origins,
while a primal flame talks stories of our ancestors.
Walking between worlds, wild & withdrawn,

bridging our discoveries with experience.
Opening to the wealth of organisms
that comprise our inheritance to live in
abundance with the whole of our being.

❧ 19 ❧

Seismic articulations of consciousness
super nova ancient stars,
breathing elements into being.
The shockwaves open pores of the fauna,
on worlds stretching across the galactic horizon.
Altering the courses of comets & rogue suns,
carrying unnamed molecules & sunsets
to unexacting solar systems.
Systems of change,
where normality never had a grasp.
Regularity peeks altering astrological clocks,
sidereal time leaps a year,
the dance of gravity & levity take turns leading.
While oceans kiss mountain peaks,
unseen volcanoes surprise the surroundings,
reframing the landscape...

꽃 20 꽃

Igniting intergalactic
I space
as pure grace.
oblong days
smoldering in the potentiality,
with one gentle word flames leap,
passions so dynamic the periodic table
fills up.
Period,
the end of infinity,
now coursing
true as a needle on North,
soul in connection with soil.
Witnessing
the delineation of sun light
to DNA, microbiomes through biosphere,
an orchestra
of cooperative organisms.
Refreshing the cultural norms.

❦ 2 1 ❦

Play,
in the animal kingdom play is archetypal.
I belong to a culture of play.
To play is to be.
Joy in the act of being.
The body breathes fully in play.

There is a problem in western culture,
possibly others,
play is thought to be for children.
This divorce is a primal cause of
distress in the western culture at large.

Where is a free association devoid of expectation
exist outside of play?
For play is not the practice of craft;
though the action of a craft may be play.

How can one expand the play in their life?
We each have areas of focus that bring our play to the forefront.

There's also an edge there,
& exploring those boundaries with play is associated with a heightened
sense of being.

In expanding our sense of awareness
of being ones experience in life becomes ever full(er).
To live a well lived life is to live a life of play.

❧ 22 ❧

Dynamic ontological explosions
of pantomimic parameters
disguised as fields of wild flowers drown out
the abysmal emotions coursing through my being.
Heretical extensions of self worth
& beliefs of friendship criss cross the narrative,
as I look on from an observers perspective.
The sylphs are flying with the harpies
swooping in for mortal blood.
Perched on a thin ledge three quarters up a sheer cliff,
they come for me,
& realize there's nothing here for them.
Gazing into their being; they see we are one,
I am simply moving slowly for my work here is yet done.
Onwards I climb to sea and to sky,
mourning humanity as I embrace this breath,
filling this vessel with spirit emerald depths.
For all who witness this self will be cast from their fog of
culture to live for a moment in the wilds of their senses.

꽃 23 꽃

Once while I was sleeping,
I saw a giant turtle who turned & smiled at me,
while it swam through a sea of stars.
It's eye was so large it dwarfed me by comparison.
Mocking birds antagonized with song in efforts to distract
me from this moment of awe;
my focus held.
Just as the giant turtle was disappearing into a galaxy not far away,
a shimmer seemed to approach me.
Growing in intensity I could feel a resonance in my core
growing in consonance.
To my delight,
this shimmer engulfed my entire visual perspective.
Here I am at peace.
Breathing in I open my eyes to begin my day.

❧ 24 ☙

There are days of wonder,
that stagger the eyes.
Causing almost hallucinations to
grasp the soul & insight a fever of awe.
Other moments of wonder are as
pits of torment & aberrations.
These bring forth a ponderance
to end all that has come before.
On occasion one is in the nether regions
between these formidable states of wonder.
Here an opportunity to tune oneself
in balance of the fulcrum.
Steady as stacked rocks in a river.
Pivotal plans for navigating are etched
in the landmarks of mind
to be witnessed during ones voyage
through the metaquantum solidity of life.
At times these landmarks are as lighthouses
when the wash of wonder has one
gasping for air.

It is here I find myself currently.

Knowing all too well the current is
sweeping me along,
& my strength is faltering.
Waves of torment & awe crushing
my neural connections,
a flash of faith shines.
Every ounce of attention twists to witness.
A voice rings out from all sides.
Perfect in polyphonic overtones
crystal cracking brilliance.
Suddenly suspended,
pierced by the tonal tumultuous,
I am,
completely captive.
Feeling cells burst in bliss,
reborn in the calm of the sun.
I am renewed with every memory intact,
a life line to a world afraid to see itself.
Naked of heart with boundaries broadcast
in the expression of eyes.
Blinking,
stretching,
I pick myself up from the salt & pepper shore
as sandpipers comb for their daily food.
Looking round,
it is time to find water & safe harbor.
With divine guidance I go forth.
Listening to each element the way is clear.

A cricket chirps.
Music of the spheres in the smallest of all.
Sacred rhythms of stars play along,
pixelating consciousness in rhymes suggest
the time is best.

25

Do you know as the feeling explodes
the ceiling when the crackle of lightening
breaks on through your perceiving.
Opens, something more for you to explore.
Is it grace that you follow,
or a harrowing silence.
Death is defying,
yet this life is abounding.
Will we ever know, or just go?
Moving faster than thunder as the shifts are a sunder,
will we fully remember
what in this world we have robbed her
& our own sense of self,
there's nothing else.
Now the stars are approaching
there's no way of knowing just a feeling is showing
as the storm keeps on growing,
yes the storm keeps on growing.

❧ 26 ☙

Curiosity doses the ephemeral
moment of our eyes gazing
into the ever shifting faces,
forever we are.
Mitochondrially exchanging consciousness,
as atoms bond in the swirl of our tongues,
giving birth to galaxies yet explored.
We circle round these suns,
orbiting infinity in this dance of curiosity.
What will be as the dawn dusks?
Unnamed tribes tumbling through a day undreamed,
giving rise to languages unheard with expressions so deep
they expose the ocean floor,
allowing them to voice emotions few now
can barely tolerate.

❀ 27 ❀

To be pursued,
even just a simple phone call or text
asking for a night together.
That is romance to me.
I desire relations that have an equality of pursuance,
on a regular yet spacious interval.
The space of connection a wild consensual sexuality.
The romance comes to life.
Dancing & grabbing, soft ephemeral caresses biting carnal tussles,
moaning ear tickling wading in orgasms.
Here a moment of pure delight
violates the time continuum
compressing infinity in these shuddering bodies,
only to be snapped back to the time and place
of the night we've traced.
Pursuing is the romance,
chasing waterfalls of amrita flowing,
stalking the subtle nuances to where these orgasms lurk,
to fountain as sweat while we melt in this feast
of sexual delight.

❧ 28 ❧

I once recalled euphoria in a state of movement.
The full release, fertility, dawns this night.
So, I pace the race, focusing with grace,
allowing ease to collide with the moment.
Full stride to achieving the mission objectives.
A cultural & species honoring of distinctions,
nurturing as an ethos of being.
Accepting the consent of trillions of organisms
flourishing as a fizzle
existing in the crackle of the universe.
Here, I dance,
extending this shedding of
traumas & misperceptions for
clear breathes of the oneness we are.
Grateful am I
for this momentary glimpse into
the majesty of this immense tapestry.

🕉 29 🕉

There's a place where the magic moment
of experiencing each other rings
the golden bell of being
in the secret heart of one another.
Samadhi mixed with nirvana dancing to the nadabrahma
of lifes chorus sung by every cell of these beings.
Presence of witnessing the divine frolic of the subtlest
movements at play in the joy of form,
woke in the wash of the world.

Brilliantly plumed birds and lizards dot the sky & landscape,
creating a theatre of natural splendor.
Dripping dreams of paisley's kaleidoscoping
with the meadows & cloud patched sky.
While dawn colours twist & metamorph with
northern lights electrifying the senses.

Here in the froth of synaptical arrangement
particles of god form &
disperse enlivening spirit in matter,

as the matter of spirit speaks through action,
birthing ecosystems of resilience
to proliferate consonance upon the planet.

Gaia, my dearly beloved!
I pray to live in a good way honoring you in all I do,
balancing morals as mortals for all this shall change.
Leave it better than I found it;...

❧ 30 ❧

I saw pentacles in aces,
as dream swept with juniper.
Infused flower, spirit, to induce the day.
For as night falls, dusk rises.
Open for unknown followings.
Entendre innuendo washes projections to be unbound.
Cured & aged to keep for eternity,
if you can manage not to eat it.
A crocodile snoring wakes,
tidal consciousness mooning, the ground soaked red.
Here we dance ablutions, cutting clothing,
shining stardust burns brightly in our eyes.
Breathing with fullness of the biosphere,
the thought of separation - hysterias.
Laughing, chortling,
rolling on the floor,
tangled in limbs ecstatic twin bliss.
Solar flares erupt streaming...
welcome surrender...
when once you came.

❧ 3 1 ❧

Life is sometimes a silent comedy.
Offerring us a perfect place to discover ourselves.

❧ 32 ❧

Pulsing with the vitality of summer
flowing through my heart.
Shafts of sunlight conjugally shifting sugars
to feed roots & stems,
Branches and body.
Tangled & trining while blindfolded & present.
Moving with ease,
while the heart radiates to the
barks gnarled edges.
Wind swept on a rock outcropping,
dreaming of the forest.
At one with Nature,
rolling on the floor,
as sun illuminates your touch,
gliding from shoulder through the opposite hip,
cartwheeling across the back,
seamlessly enraptured in this
rhythm of complimentary intuitions communicating
a body of language.

Life is fascinating.
There are so many ways we fit in or out with life.
Whether we are human, or any other species.
The question is,
how does one innovate in a box,
a structure of support, a society
- which judges books by their cover,
& people by their appearance?
As I have wrestled with this,
discovering the self of body, mind, spirit, & emotions.
Moving with nature & listening,
a sense of freshness arose.
That's why I'm here today.
Both reporting on what I've discovered &
providing an experiential play
for you to witness.

❧ 34 ❧

Sometime I like to sit,
without the barking dogs of the world
breathing down my neck.
I just want to hear the trees grow.
I want to feel the tepid earth beneath my butt.
To watch the colours of grass & moss changing
with the dappled light as woodpeckers
call in flight to hammer above me.
Clearing my passage
ways to breathe in the landscape,
taking in the acrid & decaying
nourishment of the forest floor
with the rich assortment of essential oils &
tannins of the trees.

Focusing on the present
to the mountain peeks beyond,
alighting with this winter sun.
Clouds of my emotions
contemplate precipitation

on this clear sky day.
Gently the wind gives voice
while faun & buck move imperceptibly by.
The peace here reverberates this body,
showers me in a glory to
formidable to speak of.
Here the subtlety of
Taoist Sages & Druidic Mages,
cascades a presence in
profound impressions imbibing
epiphilogical metaphor
in all aspects of the world.
The crow has ka-ed,
my time has henced I bid ado,
of my species with you...

꽃 3 5 꽃

There's only two things in this world that haunt me.
A pervasive sense of self rightness,
& a fear of excommunication.

So I call on my ability to listen,
& an unbridled connection with divinity.
Witnessing the miracle of microbes in an expression of consent,
seven generations is a wink of an eye.
Earth blinks to the galactic aristocracy &
emotions hot as a history of domination,
cooling to a present of symbiosis,
unheard in the passages of akasha,
cascading in a tesseract of infinity.

I skip rope inciting droje resonance in my auric surroundings,
cleansing this temple of flesh.

❧ 36 ☙

Once,
I dreamed, peaceful & solitary.
Until I noticed I had never been alone.
This planet is alive, & this dream is this life.
It waits patently for the dreamer to wake.
Calling out with infinite perceptions;
do you experience?
Learning happens naturally,
let laughter be the same.
Enigmatic irritations dance a delirium,
delicately deciphering symbologies narcissistically derived.
Caution is blown to the wind;
so is this planet...

Better get woke.

ॐ 37 ॐ

Bending time can be a tricky thing,
when you're caught in its warp.
Light rays tangle,
ensnaring particles in verb vibrations,
action in the stillness of it all.
Once while a wisp of consciousness snuck through,
we danced in the endlessness of it all,
pure ludus orgasms unherald in the akasha,
known only to those daring to dream
beyond the realms of imagination.
Here the courageous confound the spectators breaking
eons old paradigms for what is possible.
We give thanks for the spectacle,
as it frees us to be more than thought real.

꣠ 38 ꣠

When I dream,
I dream in colour.
Lucid in the way of a toddler,
tumbling upon each moment.
Full body breath,
invigorating each organ.
Boom!
How plentiful,
charming novelty,
rushing as a gail.
Birds singing in the vortex of annihilation.
Here in the ephemeral effervescence of ego evaporation,
all that remains is what is real.

ꙮ 39 ꙮ

Colossally igniting sacral sources,
Fluids with the Earth,
as one super organism.
Giving this love,
appreciation,
grace of movement,
to a moment of prayer
gyrated full body into the temple of our gathering.
For when we are together,
surely we are a temple,
Erecting the sacred
for receiving this divinity we bliss & sorrow
for the now to refresh & replenish,
radiating the grok of this nurturing culture.

❦ 40 ❦

Blessings my love, dearly departing,
to arrive in this heart space, embrace,
passion as subtle as the changing shades of
solar rays deep in the day.
Warmed all through the night,
holding each other as a nucleus
while we chromosomal combine.
Terra forming ecstasy,
for a generation inculcated
to balance perception with transparency.
equipped with emotion to fully know this station.
Presence in honor of Nature,
what we truly are,
planetary consciousness,
in consonance with the kingdoms,
synergy in brilliance,
as this dance elates & elementally metamorphose,
evolution through norms,
in greater coherence these moral codes give mortal souls
remembrance.

✥ 41 ✥

Wonderstruck by the innosence of this moment.
A silent space,
where bodies in motion express the essence of self
unbound by societal customs.
Free wheeling ecstatic bridging divinity with flesh,
inhabiting a primal awe of presence.
Thirsty for the twirl when our tongues twist,
helices of a romance cresting chests
nipples over lap
paradisical chakric emotions.
Fingers laced & folding,
fractals of familial lineages
accepting the dharma of their days.
Vowing to uphold this sacred charge,
through the frothy edges of infinity as
archetypes assume biospheres,
ageless animals
wrestle with forgiveness &
appreciation.

❧ 42 ❧

Drenched by the waves &
6 feet under
splashing around in these wild emotions.
Diving deeper to get below the rolling waves,
20 meters to the calmness.
Out of breath,
the light of life fills me up.
Streaking cord plasmic solar energy transmogrifying
to anchor as the crystalline core of earth.
I am riding this current as it passes straight through me.
Here in the darkness this cord is thin as a single strand,
while this play of archetypal relapse tries to cling.
Suddenly I breathe again,
electric shocks ripple through muscle,
shaking skeleton to cartilage,
golden bell rings.
Eyes open,
stinging of the sight.
A glorious day as ever,

...

❦ 43 ❦

When the battered barricades
are crumbling
in the rising tide.
Turbid are the waters
sullied by the inexorable death
brought on by the affluence of
plastics unseen by those who create them.
In a distance close enough to hear
this evisceration
of the last vestige from a society long collapsed,
a young raccoon rummages through the debris
in search of mollusks and other shell fish.
Life will persevere
even as an ecological age ends.
A mycelial matrix
now engulfs ancient forgotten city scapes,
blooming unclassified fruiting bodies
whose fragrance calls to unnamed insects
who carry these sporing mushrooms
beyond the realms of their fungal knowing.

While in flight a cousin of the swallow eats
this arthropod & regurgitates it for its young,
high upon a branch
whose trunk is twisting through the 19th floor
of a once prominent financial building.
The prolific fruits
of this stabilizing species'
pungent odor attracts
amphibians whose flight
darkens the sky at mid day.
Their song deafens
the eroding echo chamber
of incongruous architecture
where undocumented organisms cower
to evade being eaten.
High over head
vultures circle
waiting for the cast off carrion
to feast upon. & so,
another dusk has approached
on this vibrantly evolving ecosystem,
layered with centuries
of existential elucidations
engraved in archaic design
engulfed in biologies
insurmountable
parade of paradise.

❧ 44 ❧

Dominoes strike again.
Cascading into fine laced spectacle.
Releaving millennia of societal tension.
The fear of death itself extinguishes life.
The dead walk amoungst us.
A moving madness
spreading its morbidity as
progress to all they encounter.
Beyond the edges of their reach,
averting the double 9s,
I reside.
Here in a corridor glistening in ultraviolet,
rising to a fervor with particles of god.
Dancing with the senses,
I bring this life to the fallen numbers.
All I witness germinates with unstoppable
bliss.

❧ 45 ❧

Parched is the land & minds of so many.
That this drought of generations has created a culture of weak
character & inane dialogue.
So focused on the mast head
that the storm brewing off the port side
is about to overwhelm the vessel
casting all aboard to float adrift.
With a keen intuition and an ear to nature,
many are finding a renewal in their banks of perception,
alighting a kindred occupation with ancestry.
Propelled into use as appropriate technologies meet automation in an
optimized way,
so that all Beings of this biosphere flourish.
Rehydrating landscapes & minds
waiting for a culture to inspire,
beliefs put to action.
Exemplar.
The birthplace of life, water,
at one with Earth,
and a full web of spectacular diversity ebbs forth.

༄ 46 ༅

Catching the eye of ever attraction;
full engagement with the divine,
galactic ally interwoven
as molecules of burnt out suns
ignite the biochemical consciousness of
planetary awareness in every organism it holds.
In this perception
I rest with body,
emotions,
& more.
Balanced in the ever caring
nurturance of self care
witnessing all life as an aspect of self.

Fore without you I am nothing.

🎝 47 🎝

There's a moment in the polyphony of life,
while a gentle rain melts the summer heat,
that the flora breathe a sigh of relief relaxing their outstretched limbs,
and plumping subtly.
The petrichor aroma shifts the consciousness of the
fauna in this edge meadow,
forest & sea to a quiet calmness of peace
while droplets clinging to the crest of leafs slip
soundlessly on their fur & feathers bringing forth
a mild musky flavor to the milieu of aromatic euphoria
that I am so fortunate to bask in.

❦ 48 ❦

Where do the little ones go?
Those that make the flowers grow.
Those that pull the tides,
as pollen drifts back to shore,
eaten by the mussels & sand pipers
whilst a half moon glistens through the horizon.
As whales dance in the distance,
I sense magic afoot,
holding planets in orbit as
protons in a nucleus
the little ones choreograph
from a score the whales record.
Bend metal minds of bipedal trines
seeking science to explain
all that can not be seen,
yet sense must be developed
as any other skill,
the challenge is the reward.
Where do the little ones go?

Close your senses,
let your stories go,
open to the clear space of heart
where all beings are heard distinctly.
Allow the ancient threads of life to weave
us into the tapestry again.

🦂 49 🦂

Predicated on a belief,
& strung upon a high telephone wire,
where three soul searching pigeons
koo their vast epilogues in direr exasperation.
Even pigs flying is a common occurrence.
Shutter fly the night beguile,
cross sentences along the beach.
Oyster fish floundering by
dance of a tidal romance.
To speak so tongue tangled,
that novel sound expressions
tumble forth.
Contact beyond culture,
wild as life be,
this is subtle & sensitive,
even with great force.
For the force is within you,
everything that is.
Use your force to balance ones life,
recalling every life that is.

Whole body whole heart
spirit in the essence
jumping shoulders from the start,
to bending down on all fours,
giving step ups or downs when clever.

Bingo,
I off for forrest fancy.
Beliefs,
faiths up the day,
slowly devouring hypothesis
for all the possible ways,
though some are out,
& trying to creep in,
the forge is hot even quarks melt.
May you forge beliefs in such fire,
that only origins remain.

꒰ 50 ꒱

Coasting with serendipity
along the mitochondrial passages.
Free flowing energies cocreating
this fine tuning of the consciousness inherent in life,
as a human instinctive with Nature.
Full consonance inducting the heat of emotions to
cause black wholes & wormholes to
form in the calm of it all.
Vortices & portals that condense &
stretch the buddha states for all to be guided.
Great ancestors,
whose bodies balanced heaven & earth.
Being the food they eat,
light of existence
condensing as the spectrum of you.
Wonder never ceases,
when you fully witness.

51

Day light springs forth,
cresting horizons of cellulaic forms,
imbibing full spectrum life radiance.
Breathing with the panic light web,
mycelially sporing consciousness,
baring witness
in the kaleidoscopic overtonal materiality
condensing as this body.
Magma flesh scintillating senses,
overcome by the immensity of it all.
Breathing calmness to anchor
amoungst the bewildering grandeur.
Allow this full frequency to
achieve stunning radiance,
shaking out any traumas that remain.
To move fluidly,
inspired in familial relation with all that is.
Even as darkness descends,
this is ever present.

❧ 5 2 ❧

Now in the night of our love,
passions soaring as ospreys,
with home high by the sea.
Bodies in motion,
expressing the ecstatic in full being trembles
causing tectonic shifts bringing
new lands to surface &
burying cultures of unconsciousness.
These new lands give breath to
this nurturance of being,
where the iris of our eyes
reflect the truth of our souls,
springing forth to
lock thighs rough rolling
softly nibbling necks,
tantrically merged
yet spiraling through this place..

✺ 53 ✺

You know that it is,
as you let everything go.
The matter of life when living no strife,
is often a choice of perspective,
a learning directive.
That shows cooperative synergistic nurturance.
or is your whole perspective what calls,
scared of the wild forever a child,
unknowing yet seeking counter balance
levity from death.

🕸 54 🕸

The dawn of time came slowly though slowly was yet known.
To the first who perceived it,
even lightening seemed like snowflakes
drifting in a forgetful wind,
& lifetimes went by in the blink of stars imploding.
But here I recall a first breath,
as if final in the tantamount moment it was.
Pulsing vitality lit mycelial webs of neural connections,
forming thoughts as impressionistic paintings effervescing epiphanies
in the realness of the ephemeral passages.
Time,
a cruel lover,
or a nurturing companion?
Darts a course, aligned with the space between.
tic,
talk,
state your peace,
calamity, for the record.
What will be recalled of you, ancestor?
Only time will tell...

I recall the infinite,
as a deja vu,
interrupting the very pulse of my being.
Touching a core aspect of self,
reveling in a majesty of presence that humbles.
Flat upon the ground with fingers to toes,
whose body knows the fullness of awareness,
unhinged by the spectrum of separation.
To come forth a consonance
of mitochondrial connections through every cellular entity.
While light slows down to DNA.
Releasing an unheralded amount of dimethyltryptamine
in the center of brain matter,
opening eyes to the death of an ecological age.
It all, the consciousness of this time space continuum,
collapses into a quantum marble singularity

flickering into and out of existence.
I recall eternity
deja vu...

❧ 56 ❧

I cushion the passage with aggregate of hollowed out stars.
The light I am went out many eons ago,
what you see now
the shadow of light fading from matter.

The last perceptions of a figurative friend,
more like family, wells of emotions
whose depth one never imagined finishing the explorations.
But, as children
from the depths emerged again it all seems fine.
From those of us beyond the tesseract,
this time space bubble is about to burst in on itself,
having capitulated its essence to a vibration
just beyond the precipice of this time space continuum.

Loving the Now,
slowing with the growth of maple trees,
braiding shoots to play with thee,
leaving a finger print...

ABOUT THE AUTHOR

Reed Richard lives on Salt Spring Island of the Salish Sea with his family. As Conductor of OrchestraFarms.ca he is developing systems to regenerate the land & the people. An Artist of Life Reed brings a playful nurturance culture into focus throughout his creative expressions. He can be found in contact and ecstatic dance spaces & walking with the woods and waters.

To learn more about Reed and discover his current offering visit www.bendingreeds.com

facebook.com/reed.richard.5

instagram.com/bendingreeds